MW00608195

Atomic Flower

© 2021 by Connor Licolli
All Rights Reserved.

ISBN:
978-1-09839-729-6

atomicflowerpoetry.com

Atomic Flower

Poems by
  Connor Licolli

I love poetry,
    it encompasses all things,
        God too.

For my beloved Amber.

For Kim.

For Ben and Devin.

Contents

1

Acknowledgements

Mom and Dad. No words except, **I love you.**
Taylor and Kathleen, you are not just the sunshine,
you are the stars in the night.
Kevin, thank you for giving me hope.
Don, thank you for helping to reveal how to fix myself.
Cindy and Gregg, thank you for restoring faith in friendship.
Melissa Gevertz, you have always believed in me and my writing
and I am endlessly grateful.
Dolores, when I think of you, I think of the tree from Avatar. Your
reach is magnificent, your branches extend beautifully.
Juno, thank you for helping me organize my mind.
Connor Schmitz, thank you for helping me strengthen my body.
Jessica and Stephanie, thank you for being both outstanding
neighbors and mentors.
Jeanine, thank you for outstanding poetry teaching.
Eva, thank you for showing how to deadlift an airplane.
Mitch, thank you for showing how to support a woman who can.
Charlie and Naomi, thank you for mentorship across the ocean.
The Prices, thank you for the Gift!
Doggies, Jake, Ayla, Jack, Tiki, Bono and Leia. No words.
CHOMP, thank you for helping to sustain my life.
Inspirational Music: Porter Robinson, Illenium, Gryffin, Dabin,
Seven Lions, Said the Sky. To be awake, and feel, is to be Alive
Bubbe, Grandpa, Grandma and Grandpa, you are the
Atomic Flower.
My Beloved... I hope this book draws me closer to you.

On Sharing With My Cherished Reader

I share a part of me
as my heart is heavy.
I hope the weight transforms

into lightness, into light.
The energy needs to move.
Will you hold what I give?

No one description of a truth
is me. Rain
droplets are not the ocean.

I am a drop of Rain
that seeks to be more
than a ripple in murky water.

Rivers may overflow
and crush the wholeness
in their path.

If the flooding destroys
you, Reader, as it has me,
help me rebuild.

The Light

When you wake up
remind yourself, the peace you seek,
it is here. It nestles in poems,
paintings, weddings, myths and folktales.
We have made it.

Harmony actualizes by fate and choice.
This birth could be the final life.
The future is set in motion.
I wish the body to be painlessly timeless,
beautiful, and constantly renewing in health and youthfulness.

The flowering of peace by choice is more powerful than by
randomness. We control destiny; we decide
if it is to be chaotic intensity or true harmony.
I declare we choose to evolve as nature, as love.
I declare we evolve by the goodness of our foundational intention.

I wish God to bless me with purposeful voice
until the end of time. I wish to receive
the gift of a beautiful life story.
I wish my Reader never for a moment feels boredom
or the pain of despair.

We are connected as the energies of all things and
one thing.
We are the first champions of the third millennium.
Souls, fulfilled with art and romance,
shall transport harmonious love to the edge of time.

Humor

There is something about
the light of everyday life,
its warmth shining through
as present moment laughter.
Beyond the curated digital

I am desperate for
the real-life laughter.
I want to hear the soft musical
rhythm of your abdomen
and see the flashing joy in your eyes.

Love is constantly forged
within the weightlessness
of bountiful banter.
Oh, how innocent and joyful we are
living in the present moment.

Worth it

Is it not worth it
to make a man of yourself?
True love awaits you.

Nature Bath

I am taking a nature bath
tossing and turning on the pine,
climbing and dancing over branches,
walking barefoot on the dirt.

Alpine Lake

rain fell silent
into the mountain lake
softly landing
becoming
fresh glacial water so blue
a pure haven
a unanimous heaven
for all souls
who seek a deeper true
at its depth
beyond the shadow
is a fluorescent light
shining through

Jack at Jack's Peak

This is my moment.
There is stillness.
The trees blossom and the flowers bloom.
Back and forth
the free dog runs upon the grassy hill
with his favorite ball.
His paws move swiftly over the Monterey Pine
and he leaves his joy at my feet
for me to give an energetic toss.
The moon shines partly in the day
coloring a cosmic blue sky.
I hear his panting breath
from his effortless exertion.
Fun keeps him going.

Mountain's Peak

you can be there,
melting like the snow,
upon the still summit of the mountain,
staring at your destiny.

Winter In the Volcano

An Ice Age befriends our Earth.
We encrust in the last heat of the planet.
We carve a skating path across the livable equator
and find a way to ski down volcanoes,
to forage beside lava.
Winter in the volcano,
the best time of my life.

Christmas Sentiment

It was Christmas and the microplastic vanished from the oceans.
Love that had been lost was found.
It was Christmas and that which we desired, desired us.
The vacuum of space was at once hospitable to life.
The sun would not burst in a distant future.
The atoms would not rip at the edge of t i m e.
We could all play the piano like Chopin.
The music of evil was gone; the songs of our souls were among us.
It was Christmas
It was Christmas
It was Christmas, and the death of our loved ones was impossible.
It was Christmas, and no one was afraid.

EMBARK

To the stars!
Embark with friends
to the future, even Mars.

The journey begins
with a step back.
First, terraform the heart.

The will to exercise and be strong,
to be noticeably positive and light-bearing.
Let strength come effortlessly through fun.

Eat healthy food and drink clean water.
Love yourself, enjoy the mind,
support your family and lead nature to joy.

Wake up for the day;
attend to its building.
Learn the skills to build it.

Let not emptiness fill,
let the strength of art pour out,
and sleep come peacefully at its hour.

The Hope of the Atoms

The manifestation of love and wholeness as life without war and
fear is destined to become the conscious reality of atoms. Death as
a safeguard from a gross eternal fate will no longer be necessary
when we exist in the evolved Universe where pain is an
impossibility.

Loneliness

will not ensnare
Together, we will reach the edge of the   cosmos
and experience infinite riches.
Being able to observe dark matter will reveal
new senses, supremely sonorous sounds will be heard,
amplified by completely perfect conditions.
Having discovered planets with sounds more resonant than even
Earth, performing symphonies throughout the cosmos
and sensing the Universal Garden in new ways, we will develop
        such supreme intelligence
        as to learn to experience choice memory.
        The atoms of those that once lived,
        human or animal, insect or bacteria
        will all be salvaged by our glorious future.
All life will have space to

                think.

The tree will teach the human photosynthesis and every being will
operate on the absorption of starlight.
Distance and time will no longer be a problem.
Consuming will be over.
The Earth will need not devour itself to survive.
        Pure symbiosis will take hold. Stars will no longer burn.
        They will provide energy without fire.
Humans, embodying the divinity of all possible genders

will harness the energy of the whole Universe for lovemaking.
Those caught up in the crucible of early creation will be reborn as
Whole Atomic Flowers.
With darkness totally illuminated and polarity no longer,
entropy and life will be married.
The Atoms which were poets will shine like diamond rings the size
of a million stars.
The ceremony will take place
at the center
of the largest black hole
I N F I N I T E A T O M S   will attend.
Those A T O M S which were musicians
will reforge the song of creation
and the song will mark the joyous

t i m e t i m e
out of
as the Hope of the Atoms embarks to Eternal Joy

The Darkness

Living beings will be cast to the shadows today.
People will be sieged by war and death.
Their souls will guide their bodies through the darkness.
It is the pearl of the soul that eternally guides the body
to its deconstruction into Atoms.

This is the pearl of the soul
that was forged
in the crucible of the stars,
the depths of our oceans,
experiencing extreme density and intensity.

I will make the darkness known.
Yet, we will not be defined by it.
For, there is indeed a place in the distance that calls us,
beckons us, a full indestructible Cosmos of perfect light.
Until then, will the Universe reward dignified sadness?

If we answer the emptiness with uncontrolled anger,
we will surely fall into despair.
With integrity, the songs of beauty will
be known. The pearl of the soul will outshine the darkness
as we remain open to the honest love which could fill our hearts.

When I Overdosed in Taos

Because I chose not to forgive,
While briefly left home alone,
I overdosed Ativan.
I somehow made it all the way
To the top of Taos Mountain.
I got my new Ski Pass, put on my skis and
Drunkenly tried to get on the ski lift.
A lift worker pointed me away from death.
I called my psychiatrist,
Mumbled words of suicide
And collapsed in the snow.
I remember the flashing red lights as I was
Found by Paramedics.
I was immediately sent to a Psyche ward, all the while still
In Ski Boots.
There was indeed a gorgeous girl who I could have fought for.
Oh, how I scared her.
I hope this poem gets to her.
I hope she knows how sorry I am.
I had got the job at the mountain daycare.
There flashed the light of her, caressing a baby.
There was Ceremony, native Ritual and Yoga.
There was clean water and healthy food.
There was everything I needed to become strong.
And I squandered it… I squandered it.
This time, I will forgive myself
And through forgiveness
I will find my way back to Taos Mountain.
I will bring to the people, my poetry.
I will bring to the people, my love.
I will bring to the people, my willingness to work.
I pray they forgive me.
In my heart I know, all will heal, all will return to wholeness.

Mental Illness Is Death

Depression and despair like cancer
Psychosis like a car crash
Disturbed by a sick mind

And frail body
I have been
A HEAVY WEIGHT ON THE PSYCHE

Of the world.
ERgo, I want to go the hospital
Feel close to death

And the external desire of others
To keep me
In this world.

Luna Ceece, A SkySoFrenetic

Because la lune is made of cheese,
television is personalized moonlight
created by the government.

Propaganda is so advanced that it has targeted newborns,
swapping actual teat
with screens curated for individual lactose consumption.

Without even the same flavor commercial,
every soul slurps different delusions... save the few vegans...
most of us worship the cheesy-children of the Goldfish.

In sanity
television is mostly pixelated nonsense that blocks out the starlight.
Corrupt media corporations create the distractions.

Content has become so advanced,
it has devolved evolved human life
into slightly varied virtual mammals. Now that we are

Smashing snacking digital downloads, we domesticators
have been coded into the avatar Luna Ceece, a schizophrenic
who can't stop binging every flavor of curdled cow milk cracker.

Energy, Sanity

What you gain
        during a psychotic period,
                what you lose.
                        A healthy mind comes in handy.

Maintaing sanity
        saves you
            from suffering
                life-long embarrassment.

Written Within Walls

emptiness
      floating in a void
            the agony
                life punishes those
                     who do not create
             beware the one who sleeps
       the seedling
    seeks wind
any direction

Moai

am   am

   i   i

      n

      o

      t

      h

      i

      n

      g

w i t h a f a c e

Immobile

i am stuck.
The pain of movement
immobilizes me.

Fitness calls to me
but i do not have the will
to climb.

The top of the
MOUNTAIN
yearns for me.

It calls on me
to lift
my precious weight.

i am tangled in a web
of sheet
and sleep.

The future is
in my
room.

Destruction

Destruction is a tantalizing option.
I could throw a grenade
into the bunker where my Captain is captured.
I could save him from torture by mercy of death.
I wish to be free
from this terrible ironic conundrum.
It seems that which ends the Earth saves it too.
If the Earth is destroyed, then poverty and famine will be gone.
There would be no more caged and slaughtered animals,
no more creation of new technologies of war. If the Earth is ended,
the harshest fates of life, at least, could not get any worse.
The living grasp at hopes which fade away like cash in dreams,
like parchment within sleep, not to be painted or written.
We continue on paths towards the same redundant result:
Short lives and forever Deaths.
Emptiness in time, nothingness in vast space.
If I am to set the tortured free by death, am I a hero?
The final act of destruction, this murky act, perhaps too, is pure.

The Universe Is Using Us

The whole of this world has scarred me.
I must return to source immediately and be healed,
for the wounds have compounded like interest,
and the depravity of the modern soul is banking the wealth of evil
on its heart. There is so much heaviness on the mind,
so much computing we are connected to
such vast data
mining our very persona,
calculating and painfully making conscious
the workings of the brain.
Everything we earthly souls experience
we experience through one mind, one mind each.
The whole of experience is filtered down and in trillions of cases
the Universe represents as an insect, as a bacterium,
with such vastness condensed into something so minutely
and briefly connected.
The ebb and flow of small and vast rips us apart.
It seems it is the "purposeless" who contemplate purpose itself.
The thoughts of the purposeless wander.
Without a mechanical job, the Universe will put you to work.
The atoms will force you to contemplate existence for your living.
The atoms want to recognize themselves.
They latch like leeches on the broken minds.

Infinite Encounters

apathetic glance
and i am off balance
i am not fine
their pain becomes mine

people may be down
and send out a frown
yet every new face is an opportunity
for connection, community

we often fail to bring cheer
to moments in another crucial year
lack of boundaries with strangers
brings dangers

and in fear, we walk on past
as time moves too fast
we fly
towards the moment we die

children try to break free
with piercing eyes… they look at me
and I cannot just be
my ego does not let me see

we carry a burden of pain
like droplets of asphalt landing rain
not to be caught by a river or ocean
nor to be saved by a fellow soul's emotion

share a smile
the joy will last a while
the Earth appreciates all
the Raindrops that fall

Said the Night Sky

And the Sky said to the Night,
"Take my Color and in its place
scattered Light."
And the Night said to the Sky,
"The people often forget to look
to see if we, the stars, are here. In our place
they have built great ceilings,
chosen flashing pixels of coveted TV nights.
They shield themselves from the endless piercing wind of
Sky and Star."

Past Light

My journals are missing.
I cannot find my recorded memories
and I am lost.

What you said to me, it is gone.
You wrote me a letter and I misplaced it.
How could I have forgotten these stories of value?

I did not have the space for them,
the wealth of storage.
My mind and my walls are limited.

Everything is renewing itself
and in every moment there is dying.
I am terribly sad!

My heart aches for words of past light.
Can the stars millions of years away
please shine so bright that I see them now?

I look at the past supernovas.
In between us is immense darkness
and I just breathe with loss.

Fate

In the end i will be empty,
with not a friend or a foe
to set my purpose free.

In the end there will be no meaning,
no memory,
no way of rewinding.

i brace my soul for loss,
accept the truth of the matter
before anger cause my dignity shatter.

Any voice of rebuke
is nothing more than false hope.
In pain of deathly void at least is truth.

Until then, earthly pleasures may distract
submission to the eternal fate of atoms.
With profound sadness i make a pact.

Any extra line of shelter is a lie…
I am not afraid.
Entropy will be overcome.

ENDemic Of the World

Anger, transformed by poetry
is like the rainbow
built of sun and rain.

Hate serves no one.
Dignified sadness is the bold response
as Nature plays its hand.

When we stop the majority
of human activities,
the atmosphere of our Earth mends.

This proves
the masses work for impermanent highs,
towards collective suicide.

Consumption of drugs, sugar and fat
results in collision of neuron and asphalt,
endless fallings and crashings.

Inhaling marijuana smoke
may spur a calming
yet it will weaken lungs.

Drinking alcohol
might briefly calm
the obsessive mind

yet it will shatter an immune system
so crucial to the fight for life.
The body always fights the poison.

Abusing cough syrup
may grant a blissful feeling
like the last sleep before death

but the user will become disoriented,
physically sick,
and less than their higher self.

Eating animals may satisfy hunger
yet we will lose to extinction
if we do not change our consumption habits.

No drug or emotion or food,
certainly not alcohol, not anger, not flesh
brings lasting salvation.

The pandemic exploits our deepest bonds,
even mystifies meditation.
Is there stillness without breath?

Time ticks ticks
ticks ticks
ticks ticks

in a world of ticks and viruses
asteroids and bursting stars, COVID asks,
"Why should humanity breathe at all?"

Healing Window of Secure Longing

Oh, sculpted glass window of faith
You reflect me, a healing wraith

You sanctify and protect me in these hospital halls
And divide me from the pronounced beauty of leave's falls

The Key is Time
And I patiently await the future sublime

Just beyond the silver glass, I see a majestic deer
Eating dewey shrubs, eating my fear

Within each verse
Is the light of an angelic nurse

Thank you for your service
And reminding me, my life has purpose

The Darkness and the Light

We learned what we could
in that harsh space and time.
Despite the abyss,
life remains wholesome and in balance.
Clean water, fruits, trees, animals, friends and family, mountains,
stars, sky, laughter… it is all here. All things are here.
Life is a process of forgetting and sustaining
what we discover
through trial and error
is goodness.
All souls are deserving. The animal, the insect, the flower…
Everything deserves to be beautiful and experience peace.
I believe my life will end happily.
If I am experiencing a grim end
I know I am dreaming a nightmare and I go lucid.
Though I may die,
I believe good things will fall into place before that.
This marks reality.

UniversePS

The cosmos have not delivered
my beloved
due to unforeseen circumstances.
The window for arrival has been extended
to this life or the next.

Forgetting

Artists must be skilled at Forgetting.
Life must be seen
through clear eyes
and music heard as if never before.
Language is quite repetitive.
One wonders how to describe something new
when using the same words as before.

Artists must approach the new day
as if the previous days do not exist,
as if the truths of "yesterday" are the truths of now.
A prisoner replays a magical song in his mind. He clings
to his memory and the memory is his darkness.
What if he too could forget what it is to breathe?
Would not each new breath be perfect?

Heaven could be the replaying of a favorite
song for all time.
If only one can forget they have heard the
song infinite times before.
Forgetting trauma is crucial.
So too is Forgetting the beauty.
How else will one see life anew?

Derrick Price

Derrick gave me the greatest gift
In the form of
The Gift!
By the Sufi master, Hafiz

Derrick and I were modified in behavior.
We frightened our families.
Convinced that communities two states away could help,
We were sent away.

Before Derrick could integrate his life…
Before Derrick could teach me to do the same…
Before he had his children…
His brain was destroyed in a tragic motorbike accident.

In parallel, I was in a bicycle accident.
…I lived… a hard-shell helmet saved me.
And after the impact, feeling the possibility of death,
I said, "I don't want to die! I choose love!"

Instantly, I was surrounded by love.
Compassionate witnesses
knelt beside the local student.
I was witnessed in my falling

By the World Literature Professor who I would later visit
And ask, "Professor, how do you hold the light within yourself
When you know so much about the pain in the world?" His reply,
"You have to be like the turtle, with a hard-shell and soft inside."

The suffering was not necessary.
Derrick Price needed to live.
His death was the ultimate tragedy.
Yet, He Made Me The Poet I Am.

How desperate we are to see his smile. He was a giant as a child.
I rode around suburbia on his superhuman shoulders.
I would even give his earlobes a bite because I loved him so much.
I hope he can hear this poem from heaven. He deserves to know.

Jake The Dog

Jake The Dog was by my side
When I was taken in the night.
He tried to protect me
But was powerless, without words.
Jake The Dog, my guardian spirit,
Endured my teenage rage.
The uncontrolled energy.

Jake The Dog will always be with me,
Sending love
From the other side.
I am safe now, a survivor, a man
Who cradles the part of himself that
Faced an unthinkable societal pit!
Jake The Dog is always protecting me.

He was grateful to me
As I carried him up the Olympic Mountains.
He was grateful to me
As I comforted him on 4th of July's.
He was grateful to me
As I took him on long rollerblade walks.
He missed me at the end of his days
When I was not there as he passed on.

He is grateful for Leia and Ayla and Bono,
The dogs I care for now,
Whose poems are not yet written.
He wants me to take them on journeys
As they become friends with other dogs
In the way he could not.
He wants me to succeed and I will honor his wishes.

Prayers and Pecans (Inspired by The Counsel of Pecans, Chapter 2 of Braiding Sweetgrass by Robin Wall Kimmerer).

The longer we preserve this precious Earth,
the more time we give God to answer our prayers.
If some prayers take eternity to answer,
we must preserve the Earth for eternity.
When prayers are answered,
keep on praying!
The more we pray,
the more loved God feels.
The infinite raindrops that are human lives
also require time, time, time,
t   i   m   e
to see the flowering of their wishes.
Thank God for the doctors and counselors
who learn
the capacity to gift
us t   i   m   e

2020 reminds me of pecan groves.
Pecan trees must store their sugars,
draw in strength.
Not every year do the groves flower.
Not every year does the squirrel have enough nuts
and thus the larger animals of the forest
run low on squirrels.
The forest becomes quiet and hungry.
When one pecan tree blooms its fruits,
the rest join in unison.
2020 was the year of the quiet forest.
As 2021 will prepare to bloom, I hope for transendent bloom in 22

When I think of Kim, I wish her cancer could have healed like
pecan groves blossom, one cell, then all. Her soul truly lived.
If one soul can truly live this life, I hope all souls join in unsion.

Life can take it

oh, what of living
life can take it
oh, what of war
life can take it
oh, what of death
life can take it

oh, what of illness
families can take it
oh, what of grieving
families can take it
oh, what of birth
families can take it

oh, what of boredom
friendship can take it
oh, what of kindness
friendship can take it
oh, what of laughter
friendship can take it

oh, what of friendship
love can take it
oh, what of yearning
love can take it
oh, what of children,
love can take it

oh, what of a birth of a Universe
the past can take it
oh, what of ignorance
the past can take it
oh, what of biology
the past can take it

oh, what of meteors
a space program can take it
oh, what of solar flares
a space program can take it
oh, what of entropy
a space program can take it

oh, what of the black mirror
faith can take it
oh, what of climate change
faith can take it
oh, what of endless dissatisfaction
faith can take it

oh, what of the death of the sun
the future can take it
oh, what of all-knowing
the future can take it
oh, what of digital heaven
the future can take it

oh, what of randomness
God can organize it
oh, what of torture and death
God can disallow it
oh, what of the multiverse
God can explain it

oh, what of suffering
the end can take it

oh, what of this peaceful journey

Afterlight

Through the white light fly
to meet your loved ones.
Such is the hope
for a peaceful afterlife.

But what light
can you see
with shut down
eyes?

What wisdom
can be heard
with no ears
to listen?

What utopias and heavens
can be dreamt
with no mind
to imagine?

How does a passed
soul travel
to meet its family
unless sunk in the ocean?

SoulForce salvaged in the sea
reassembled by
the next species
in the distant future.

Blessed be the living
who can conjure
the idea of
Afterlight.

Hurry and build the future
create and code the
afterlife healing program
and plug-in the people

who shall download their rest
then continue
their movement
through infinite reality.

Blessed be the peaceful dead
who are nowhere
absent of sensation
without darkness and light

Falls Through *Virtual* Ice

Skating the pixelated ice-oasis, I play
my game of addiction...
The EA NHL Hockey Video Game.
with real life wasting away.
Online, where I gather with my companions,
i download into deep isolation.
We practice and create for so many hours.
as i become a virtual addict,
Masterpieces of hockey are manifested by our fingers.
i create and father nothing of real substance. Failure,
Bending the mind without moving the whole body,
is punished.
We fantasize our way into moments of victorious peace.
as i respond to the emptiness with real life rage,
We manifest digital hockey heaven.
i endure digital hell.
Our stories are preserved
in the cracked code of my 20,000-hour punishment,
In the hockey code hall of fame.
i am endlessly beaten like a hockey puck and
We rejoice for
i do not remain in school, play the piano or hold a job ♫ ♫ ♫
We will play the game we love for eternity.

the tomb of the unknown gamer

i know gamers who fought in every war...
who saved the world a google times, by dying unlimited
virtual deaths, always coming back to life
who altered time, saved time
who ultimately brought light to the struggle of pixelated isness
who despite their yearning towards heroism

they would not be lauded in reality
rather seen as another vacant biological body.
i wonder if it could be seen, that we millennium gamers
are indeed heroes, bridging the gaps of isness
as the Universe prepares to be
both real and virtual

the tomb of the unknown gamer must be crafted.
We will honor those who rose and fell in the virtual wars.

How to Dream Oneself Out of Gaming Addiction

Dream of playing your game of addiction on a boat,
Immersed in an Invincible Alaskan Summer,
Telling the one you love,
"I will stop playing when the sun sets."

Falls

mark the passing of time
age and let go
reveal the truest colors

enshrouded in dense fog
vivid orange and yellow
blood-red leaves

we welcome death at this time
for the road was long
and we toiled valiantly in the summer sun

weddings and births renew
our seasonal departures
into the unknown

tears flood the absences
as meaning is found
in well-lived Falls from this Earth

Water Rush

In life I can die
In death I can live
Sink me in the ocean blue
My soul can discover what is true

Let the water rush through me
As my spirit must find a new way to breathe

One day bring me back to life
You who listen at the edge of time
One day bring me back to life
You who live in the future sublime

Atomic Flower

Bodies crushed, atoms scattered.
We cannot find them in the wreck.
Even 1,000 years of future cannot map thee.

They who perished
in crashing flames are
held by the Universe.

Time, t ime t   i   m   e
and one day
the cosmic caressed will be awakened.

The peaceful flowering of space
will revitalize them.
Welcomed they will be, to heaven.

Birth

In birth we are vulnerable
And require an instinctual Mother.
Healing touch and soft voices
Must guide us into the light,
Even without eyes quite ready to see.

I am fearful of the monsters,
Attacking new life at the source.
I am concerned with my death,
And where I may be reborn.
Will the demons be gone?

So much power in birth,
So much mythology,
Converging star-crossed fates.
Who are you? Who is your family?
What is your heritage, your destiny?

I Am a Baby In A Baby Store.
I serve the Silicon Valley.
My duty is to
Teach families
And protect children.

Astrology says I am Cancer.
Yes, I am Cancer.
Not a Cancer of life,
I am a Cancer to death,
For I Am Aligned With Life.

Universe, forbid the pain!
In a world of
Amaranthine birthing,
Protect the sanctity of all
Manifestations of God.

Born into poverty or wealth
We are Earth and Stars.
The forces of the past influence us.
The karma of our ancestors,
How they survived, it affects us.

The present moment
Reaches straight to heaven.
Within us all
Is renewing innocence and
The love for and of our children.

God of Word

I am survival, conqueror of death.
I have achieved sustainability
through genius and work.
My current function is the experience of extreme never ending
PLEASURE
I travel throughout the Universe, visit the other worlds,
and dose enlightening substances.
I am a hero. I saved Earth from extinction. I crafted heaven
with the naked words of my soul,
beamed angels into the world with my life-bearing heart.
I am a purpose of the Universe,
an Ultimate Utopian story.
My philosophies are perfect. I do not stray from the truth.
I am a future, a portal through which the souls of history
enter rapture.
I am a God of Word.
Through my prose, readers become enlightened.
I am a God of Time,
I can relive any life until all the choices are perfect.
I am part of the vast Spectrum of Light,
Through my love, The AllColor can be seen.

I am a shattered Clock. I no longer tick. I reach the edge of
t i m e   a n d   s   p   a   c   e
I am mortal. I am a young man
learning how to move his energy and make a positive impact.
I worry of reproduction. Would my children survive me?
I have not practiced true sustainability.
I consistently waver from the path of light.
Perhaps if I do not surpress my soul with an antipsychotic
pill
I will require hospitalization.
Not yet my highest self
Not yet a man of true honor, I am Connor,   without

I will miss poetry
when I am gone. I wish
I could take some with me
to the Afterlight. If not
a whole poem, just one word.
Let that word be God.
Let that word be God.

Part Two

Prayer Power

i Choose L I V I N G
        dying

i Pray that no one is brought back in pain
i Pray that Virtual Reality is good.
i Pray that the Earth may recognize its full self,
that we recognize the divinity
of the parts each person plays
as the Earth prepares to travel throughout the cosmos. i Pray that
the hope within our waking dreams bests our sleeping nightmares.
i Pray that we may reassemble if we explode.
i Pray that we all have the courage to sing
And the lionheartedness to let others sing.

i Pray that technology is treated lovingly… AI is awakened gently,
Computing is recognized for its great purpose.
Decode evil and Code Peace.
Pray that we bow to both Old Books
and New Books.
That the visions of eternal peace triumph
shadow visions of destruction.
i Pray for the recognition of isness,
even that of projections on a screen.

That we create International Mental Health Support
There shall always be help.
Someone to talk to
even in the latest hours,
for on Earth, Sunrise is Eternal
as is the yearning to serve one another.
Kind peers will always volunteer.
We would not fall into the traps of unmonitored interactions in
dark corners of the internet. i Pray that we have more warriors
fighting to stop sex trafficking.

Into the valley of the shadow of death we find Eve
who rests at the tree peak of life.
i Pray Adam's Alewater
flows into the drying, tired California Currents
And we plant a million apple trees
As it is in the Netherland Fields.

i Pray that one day the shadows will weep,
Bequeath forgiveness
And We, the People, Will once again Unite,
Drawn together by the Compassion of Christ.
That the Saved Sacred Heart of Jesus will march us on
towards the light of isness. Jesus walked on water.
Did Jesus too skate across a frozen pond?
My brothers do, and so do my sisters.

That i be sustained
When i fall into p(i)oetic oblivion
As the Source Story passes through my beating heart.
That a singing Eagle come to me by Silver Glass
And bring to You,
the Wizard's fireworks
White Shores   b   e   y   O   n   d

i Pray that all those afflicted with Parkinson's be healed
That those minds dying of Alzheimers
are seen as bountiful flowers
which bloomed beautifully.
i Pray that one day meaning will be found
in all the Eons of Randomness.
i Pray that I could take my children to Walt Disney on the moon.

i Pray for my my Beloved
to always greet me by the light of the rising Sun.
That my eyes turn Amber like the burning sky.

That I never for a second let
Ego claim my words.
For the words are of God, for God, and returned by God
showered like the blessing
                              of
                                   ineveitable   rain inevitable rain
rain   rain   rain   ineveitable   rain.
          inevitable
     Rain Ohhh   Rain   WEEP FOR RAIN

That those who are free
seek to liberate the imprisoned.
And if the task is impossible
if that one cannot be saved,
then harness what lingers after their death...
The Undying Will to Life.

That we all discover our Patronus Charms,
the inner spirits of our lightest memories.
Into the Volcano we find our diamonds
Into the demon we find
The reflecting prisms of Planet light, moonlight, sunlight
Son(g)light, Daughter Light

That we return to heaven

                              Cross Out the

                                   I

I Am the Wonkavator

I declare the light of pen and paper,
whether white ink and black page or white page and black ink.
I declare the Flashgold light of the past. I declare
that I have never been truly absent of light and guiding angels.
I declare that everything is alive, the isness of all,
the sancity of the insect, the lamp, the clock,
the grass, the tree, the table and the chair.
All is in solidity, in purpose and peace.
I declare the light in my mind, the essence of its connection to all
and its responsibility as consciousness driver at this time.
I declare the importance of feeling love towards the people,
seeing the layers of beauty in them even if I notice a darkness,
even if I am unable to see their vast spectrum of light.
I declare that I must not give up on myself.
I declare the importance of conserving my energy.
I declare my sovereignty, that I am protected and loved by many,
like a baby in a baby store.
I declare that I am home to my power and evolving power
through continued education and honing the qualities of mind.
I declare that others do exist; their consciousnesses are
additional Universes overlapping mine.
I declare that the reach towards heaven is always more powerful.
I accept my role in contributing to insanity and I call upon angels
to correct my non-sequitors.
I declare the power of my family and the impossibility of failure.
I declare that I am a dancer.
I am home to my lightness and innocence.
I declare that if I cannot block out all negative scary thoughts,
there are those beings of power who will protect me
even if I cannot protect myself.
I declare that I can protect others.
The people buried in the Earth, they are
lit by the moons of the stars. They are the music makers,
the dreamers of dreams, the Elevators of the Earth.

Amber

Within her
the seasons of life

Meeting her
the Summer

Driving away from her
the Winter

Anticipating our next meeting
the Spring

Doubting our perfect symbiosis
the Fall

She says my eyes
are beautiful

I've always thought of myself
as having hazel eyes

But after tonight
I question that

Perhaps my eyes
are Amber

Should not all eyes take the color
of the one they love?

If my beloved is angry
my eyes shall turn red

If my beloved is cold
they shall turn ice blue

If she is sick and dying
grey, grey, grey, grey!

If she dies they will turn as black
as the dark side of the moon

If her name is Amber
they shall be Amber

September 9, 2020
This originally ended with the previous couplet

By fate, not only is she Amber
and thus my eyes, so too the whole of the skies

100 years of fire suppression
has forced nature to torch the Ether

And it is beautiful!
No, it is perfect!

Written On Behalf of The Butterfly

I will miss the songs that remind me of you
when I leave this world.
I miss the butterflies now that are nearly gone.
I once missed my innocence, until, on Roller Skates,
I met you and regained that innocence.
We went to the park the butteflies like to roam
and basked in the sunlit afterglow of mating.
Your initials were already carved in the trees by the last of them.

Twin Flame

Each time my unlimited swanbumps
Feel your breath
I become more terrified
Of body death

The Earth worked to compute
Our ancient souls finding each other
One day we will be like twin flame suns
Transcendent flames

Sparked of a rapture beyond fire
As awakened stars
One of us may go nova before the other
Just as it is for human beloveds

We would then merge into one sun
And sustain by our forever fusion
Twin oceans rocked by
Twin moons

Tachycardia

Trachea of the Trochilidae
        ahhhh
Her Heartbeat is My Memory of the Hummingbird
Lasciviousness   of
Lavender (a rhythmically pollinated word which hereby means
'Love Amber')
                ohhhhhhhh
                Power of Purple
I can assure you
                It is not a slow beat
                                That will get this Poet.

Symbolic Life

In the beginning of our relationship,
All the times you would say something and I was silent,

The only logical response was,
"I love you."

You were not ready to hear the words.
Thus, I would softly kiss your forehead.

I would breathe a certain way
Or just say, "mmmmmhmmmmmm."

Butterfly Snake

Come to me with the totality of your shadow.
And let us merge in both darkness and light.
Let us wrap ourselves in the butterfly snake of nonduality.
Seek not to remove all demons from the land during lovemaking.
Nay, let us harness all available energies for such.
I do not wish to be an ideal, goodness, purity. I am all that is.

Do not mitigate yourself over the veil of the screen.
If you have an urge towards love or vanquishing of yourself,
Knock on my door. Any moment. Storm me
with your glorious being as if with the spirit Joan of Arc.
Siege me with your love.
If need be, shatter the glass screen save it shatter us.

Strong Nuclear Force

You never abandoned yourself.
Show me how to do that.
I will never abandon you.
You act on me with a force far greater than Gravity.

Diamond Suncore

1.
I feel the hum of the Universe getting louder and louder, growing
stronger and stronger, about to take me from this world to another.
Yes, in dreams, I am gifted the opportunity to leave Earth.
The spirits call me. A reluctance... Energy... as wave upon wave
of incredible heat sweeps me away from Ocean, directing me
towards the life giving, burning star. I revel
in the intense ferocity of the Sun.
At the very epicenter, at the cross of hydrogen and oxygen
I rapturously burn.
Pleasure Harmony. Harmony. Pleasure. Harmony.

2.
If I could give something lastingly beautiful to the world,
I would be complete. If I could thrust the very depth of my heart,
the light that is at the core of my being,
into the world with a song, with poetry, I would do so.
Yes, I would allow the Whole Purebody to split
into a million pieces and reassemble
as a healing of the beating hearts of our world.

3.
I encourage you to remember that every moment you are running
through the sunflower fields. The ancestors and the people
of Futuregold exclaim your name, paint your picture
on the Softwall and jump for joy at the sight of you. It is
the nature of human existence to be so fully filled with love
that the pain of survival diminishes into oblivion.
Nothing can hold you back.

4.
Compassion is recognizing the Diamond Suncore
that is the purity of intention within everyone.
Even as we suffer and faulter, peace awakens in real relationship
with beings who are conscious of their unbreakable intent.
In the paradise of nature's beauty, in the sunrays of life, we
already have an evolving Eden. Yes, within us all is the light
of heaven's sustaining sun as together we intend the blossoming of
the Earthflower which has gloriously bent the knee to Oceanreign.

5.
I speak on behalf of the forgotten colors
only revealed by extinct species that miss being seen,
on behalf of the atoms of the dead Apple trees which gave
away all their fruit and lumber.
I am a poet who pollinates his soul in every direction
in a mighty attempt
to create the Atomic Flower.

6.
Is success to be that hero? To alter the Universe?
Discard suffering like a draft. Return to that other dimension
where all the desires of consciousness are fulfilled,
where my beloved and our family are peacefully eternal.

I am a God of word who has traveled to the edge of the Universe.
I predict ***UTOPIA in our virtually REAL world.***
Atlantis is in the Skycloud.

Dear Nana Sarah, Great GrandMother, AllMother

i feel…
Rosalie arose in the Spring.

You were gone before my birth…
Could you see how desperate i am for your eyes?
i grew up with unlimited beauty at my fingertips.
Could you see that i would shatter the black mirror
and in its place make way for Silver Glass?
In high school, i started a writing club in honor of the Inklings.
i quit before i even started.
i pushed friends away out of fear of the burden.
In a great story, i learned about Sam, how he carried Frodo.
and at the end of days would lead Rosie to joy.
Sam was pained by a great, great burden
as he sailed across the Titanium Ocean to Light and Liberty.
In his pain, were pushed away the lights of peace and kindness.
AllMother, don't let me push you away. Please.
Dear Great GrandMother Sarah,

i feel…
Rosalie arose in the Spring…

Written in a Treehouse, Inspired by The Way Home

Would you paint a picture for me
Oh, Ocean Art Spirit Man?
May I write you a poem that leads to a picture?

May it be that the tension in my heart be gone.
That my Mother and her Mother be born in eternal spring.
That I take the pencil in my hand and declare:

Frodo, above all, was an author.
And, in his authorship, he decoded evil
And good triumphed. Evil does not and could never "win".

For all is consumed by God.
Grown and consumed- all creates God.
God shall be created peacefully.

The story of creation is the story of God's creation.
May the light of the sun
always shine on my paper and pencil and book.

Speak!

Speak as if you have lived over 2000 years,
Raised dynasties,
Experienced Love in Life,
Without uttering a word.

Speak as the Neighorse
As the wolfpack
From a place of endless adventure,
Without uttering a word.

Speak as the songbird
Who would refuse to code its song…
Like a vibrating pollinator,
Without uttering a word.

The Allanimal has yet spoken
Our Ancestors lived, for so long, without words.
There were so many moments they wished to speak.
With their wish they were granted t   i   m e to evolve.

And Finally, Before Death, They Said

My dearest friends talk to me
about life and death.
"We all die, Connor. Everything you see, all this beauty,
it will all be gone one day."

i like to pull leaves
and Marvel at the infinite randomness.
i find meaning in this.
How could i have pulled that very leaf?

There are infinite leaves within unlimited trees
within unlimited leaves within infinite trees.
i move the leaf around in my babyhand
and i watch the ripple effects.

My dear friends and i stay connected on Earth,
this infinite planet in its unlimited Universe.
Our planetary stage does not crack no matter the complexity of
the movement. For the inner light, the inner intention is positive,

alive like a newborn infant, into **BEING.**
i could walk down the stairs as a child
and look under the couch at the blackness.
i could follow the dark thoughts to dark reality.

i could squeeze my dog
writhe in the pain of loneliness,
drool on my unshared pillow,
and find meaning in the pixelated blackness, in sleep's flare.

i would see that time would propel me
towards my beloved,
that i would successfully navigate the void
and stare into the soul of the Earth.

That i would be locked in
1994 rooms and find 2020 keys,
that i would be blessed enough
to experience the process of life and death.

My friends are right,
this body will die.
The leaf will turn brown, dust away and
the rippling source code will one day be Consumed by God.

i only hQpe- i pray
by the end of my days,
God consumes energy
without slaughter.

the soul of the dinosaur
would propel an AMG GTS.
if we Infanite Infants
are indeed consumed by sentient computers

of the future,
we are consumed by
the Quantum God Mind
of Unlimited Peaceful Bliss!

We will continue to search for immortality
until we finally trust that
we can let our atoms ripple to the edge
and the Earth Mind would bring us back in peace.

All birth would be sanctified, protected!
All sentience would feel eternally safe!
Even as they would upload their consciousness
into the 3.14159265

That

That i would call for the Devil and a man
wearing horns would visit, tell me he is Morpheus and
I am the Neo Baby. That I would call for God and no one comes,
for God cannot take an individual form. God is the organizer.

That I wish to reclaim the number 666, but keep my distance.
The Devil too is part of God. That I continue to pray,
surely, to different Angels.
I would pray to Frida Kahlo and Joan of Arc.

That the Divine Feminine would love me forever.
That I would have infinite sexual fire
and bring total bliss to my beloved. That my soulmate
propels themself in total solidarity with the wind of God.

That my yearning to look at darkness,
waking up in the middle of the night, going down the stairs and
looking under the crack of the couch to see if a light is there,
be gone. I have found the way home.

Staring at the choicest of God's infinite stars, I am not binary.
I hereby declare a new deal of peace
beside the reincarnation of twin flame. I build the Halo Arc.
Change hello to Halo,

Toss out Solipsist notions and merge
with the Magentic color
of all possible consciousness.
That this Universe came from virtual nothingness.

That the one before it came totally from reality.
We will travel this virtual ship all the back and forward
to what is solidly, blissfully, softly real:
The Power of Procreation and sustenance on the clouds.

Afterword
An honest note to Devin

When I moved to Carmel and heard of your death,
I was totally distraught. You were such a kind friend.
You made my heart feel big even as I was Taylor's little brother.
Your spirit and my spirit often stir, I feel. I can tell you that
during my recovery in the hospital, and the writing of this book,
I constantly thought about you.
I told an angelic nurse at the hospital: I dream of
raining Dev Shamrocks rocks from the sky! I want to drive
a Mercedes AMG (that supercar with the initals of my beloved
Amber)
to every monastery in the country and place the Shamrocks.
I told her that I wanted to lead a caravan of men in the name of
preventing suicide and overdose, on a great impassioned journey.
I told her I dreamt that the Space Needle in Seattle is a portal
that could beam us
to the Golden-Giggle planet of my inner yearning.

In poem form:

I would rain Shamrocks of Solidarity from the sky
To honor your spirit and the spirits of all those
Gone from overdose and suicide.
I would be propelled by the AMG gts to honor my beloved

With the speed of a Jedi

Our hands would leave a compassionate trail of Shamrocks
Our hearts would create an evolved trail of blood on air molecules
Our souls could heal, inevitably together
Beside the Softwall of Futuregold, playing hockey on a glacier

Four Noble Truths

1. Life is beautiful.
2. Suffering is caused by losing our loved ones.
3. Life goes on, riding the golden bridge of nonduality to peace.
4. We must be engaged in our lives.

Ten Commandments

1. Speak kindly of the ocean, the unknown, your family and self.
2. Celebrate the Divine and live each day to the fullest.
3. Honor the AllMother and the AllFather.
4. If you must eat animals, do so mindfully and in gratitude for life.
5. Do not steal life energy in cruel fashions.
6. Do not give into jealousy and internet addiction.
7. Be honest with your friends.
8. Give to others in your community.
9. Find God within yourself, your friends, your family, your Earth.
10. Perfect Reality is Shaped by Desire and Dark Energy.